Contents

Any words appearing in the text in bold, **like this,** are explained in the glossary. You can also look out for them in the Word Bank box at the bottom of each page.

Roar of the crowd

Black Death

The **plague** known as the "Black Death" arrived in Florence in 1348. Some of the terrible symptoms were huge lumps either between the thigh and the body, in the groin region, or under the armpit; a sudden fever; and blood in the **saliva**. Before it died down, this deadly disease wiped out half the city's population.

You wake up in a hotel room with a high ceiling. The sheets are crisp and white, and the furniture is made of dark, heavy wood. The floor is covered in tiles. When you put your feet down, they feel lovely and cool on such a hot June day. But where are you? Time to get up, go outside, and investigate!

As you leave the hotel, you turn a corner. Before you have time to think about where you are, you see something crazy going on at the end of the street. It looks like a weird game of football, but with the players dressed in **medieval** clothes. There don't seem to be many rules, either!

Some of the tackles in Florence's *Gioco di Calcio Storico* can get quite aggressive, despite the old-fashioned costumes!

WORD BANK   architect person whose job it is to design buildings
medieval period from between about AD 500 and 1500

This crazy game is the *Gioco di Calcio Storico*. You wander up to the watching crowd, and someone explains that it is an ancient kind of football tournament. Teams from the four quarters of the city play one another. The matches are part of one of the city's festivals, the Festival of Saint John. But which city are you in? "Florence, of course – the greatest, most beautiful city in Italy!" replies one of the other spectators.

The *duomo*

The *duomo*, or "dome", of the Church of Santa Maria del Fiore is the most famous sight in Florence. When it was planned in 1294, no one had any idea how it could be built! The dome was finally finished many years later in 1436.

Inside the Church of Santa Maria del Fiore is the tomb of Filippo Grunelleschi, the **architect** who finished the dome. He is the only citizen of Florence ever to be buried there. ►

plague disease that spreads quickly and affects a lot of people
saliva watery liquid produced in your mouth

Regions of Italy

Back at your hotel, you find something you missed as you rushed out this morning. It's a map, left behind by another traveller. What's even better is that they have left photos and have also added labels, explaining the different areas of Italy.

Italy fact file

POPULATION:
57.4 million

AREA:
301,245 square kilometres (116,311 square miles)

RELIGION:
many people are Roman Catholic

LANGUAGE:
Italian

CURRENCY:
Euro

TYPE OF GOVERNMENT:
democratically elected

The sun-baked southern regions of Italy produce the ripest crops. The climate is so good that some tropical fruit can be grown!

Market stalls selling fresh fruit and vegetables can be found on every street corner in Italy.

Italy is famous for its fashionable clothes and world-class designers. Milan Fashion Week is a showcase for hundreds of designer collections, ranging from Calvin Klein to Giorgio Armani. Within weeks, the expensive designs are in the shops and ready to wear!

WORD BANK democracy where the people of a country elect their government

Northern Italy is the wealthiest part of Italy, and some of the country's grandest cities are here. Regions such as Emilia-Romagna – which is where spaghetti Bolognese comes from – are famous for their great food.

Central Italy is best known for its beautiful countryside, especially in the Tuscany region. Some of the small towns here are among the oldest in Italy, and are also very beautiful.

The mountainous border regions of Italy blend with neighbouring countries. Alto-Adige, on the border of Austria, only became part of Italy after World War I. Some people there still speak German instead of Italian.

The South is sometimes called *il mezzogiorno*. Some of Italy's poorest regions are in the south. Many people still work on small farms and earn only a little money. Cities such as Naples and beauty spots such as the Amalfi Coast attract many visitors.

Sicily is closer to Africa than it is to the Alps. Its buildings, cooking, and people all show traces of North African influence, especially in the west of the island.

SWITZERLAND
AUSTRIA
ALPS
DOLOMITE MOUNTAINS
SLOVENIA
Lake Como
CROATIA
Mount Bianco
Mount Rosa
Milan
Po river
Venice
BOSNIA-HERZEGOVINA
Turin
FRANCE
Bologna
Arno river
Florence
Pisa
Tuscany
Tiber river
ADRIATIC SEA
Siena
APPENINE MOUNTAINS
SERBIA
Rome
This is the heel
Naples
SARDINIA
Pompeii
Mount Vesuvius
Herculaneum
This is the toe
Cagliari
TYRRHENIAN SEA
This is called the "boot" of Italy!
Palermo
Mount Etna
FAVIGNANA
SICILY
Agrigento
ALGERIA
MEDITERRANEAN SEA
TUNISIA

N
W   E
S

0   300 km
0   200 miles

History of Italy

Florence

You are here!

ROME

N
W • E
S

0   150 km

0   100 miles

The city of Florence existed long before the country of Italy was founded. The great Roman general, Julius Caesar, founded Florence as a home for retired soldiers in 59 BC. Later, in 49 BC, Caesar became **dictator** of Rome and ruler of the Roman **Empire**.

At that time, the Roman Empire controlled much of Europe. Under Caesar's leadership, Roman armies conquered large areas of western Europe. They even controlled the ruler of Egypt, as well as areas of North Africa and even parts of Asia.

The Roman grid

The centre of Florence was laid out in a grid system, which the ancient Romans often used. This is a type of city plan where the streets run at right angles to each other, forming a grid. A similar system is used today in US cities such as New York and Chicago.

Members of the Roman Senate stabbed Julius Caesar to death in 44 BC. The senators feared Caesar was about to make himself king of Rome.

WORD BANK   assassinate to kill or murder someone
dictator ruler who has complete power over everything within a country

Caesar became so powerful that other leaders were worried he would declare himself king of Rome. Rome was a republic, which meant that the people in Rome chose their own leaders. Many Romans hated the idea of a king who could pass on his power to whomever he liked. In 44 BC, Caesar was **assassinated**, mainly to stop this from happening.

The Roman Empire existed for hundreds of years, but finally ended in AD 476. Even so, there are lots of reminders of the Roman Empire around today:

- Many courts and laws around the world are based on the Roman legal system.
- Roman **architecture** has influenced the design of many famous buildings.
- Many of the words we speak first came from the Roman language, which was called Latin.

The Renaissance

The Renaissance – or "rebirth" – tried to recreate some of ancient Rome's ideas in art, literature, and **architecture**. It began in Italy in the early 1300s and spread all around Europe. The Renaissance lasted for almost 200 years.

The US White House, completed in 1800, was designed in a Renaissance style, mixing ideas from ancient Greece and Rome.

empire group of countries controlled by another country

A young country

The Santa Croce district of Florence, where you are staying, has always been famous for big public events. At different times between 1434 and 1737, members of a family called the Medici family ruled Florence. The Medici used Santa Croce Palace for great celebrations of their rule.

Between 1494 and 1498, a Christian **monk** named Savonarola ruled Florence. Savonarola used Santa Croce for public **executions** of "heretics" (people who did not agree with his version of Christianity). Their blood soaked into the same ground where the footballers were playing this morning.

► Monuments to the Medici family, who ruled Florence for hundreds of years, are everywhere in the city.

WORD BANK

execution   killing of someone on the orders of the government or a ruler
monk   man who lives in a religious community, devoting his life to religion

A divided land

The monk Savonarola ruled in the days when Florence was a powerful city with its own laws. Back then, Italy was not yet one country. Instead it was divided into separate areas with different rulers.

A united Italy

At first, only northern Italy was part of the new country. In 1860 a man named Garibaldi led a group of volunteers (called the Redshirts) from the north to the island of Sicily in the south. The Sicilians had rebelled against their rulers and demanded to join the new country of Italy. Then Garibaldi crossed back to the mainland and captured southern Italy, too. By 1861, only the cities of Rome and Venice were not part of Italy. Italy was finally a united country.

The Redshirts

Redshirts was the name given to a thousand volunteers who sailed to Sicily in 1860. They got this name from the red shirts they always wore. The Redshirts were originally members of a group of **nationalists** called the "Italian Legion".

Garibaldi leads the Redshirts ashore at Sicily in 1860.

nationalist someone who wants his or her country to have its own government

11

Landscape of Italy

A volcanic land

Mount Etna in Sicily is one of the world's largest volcanoes, at 3,325 metres (10,952 feet). Etna is unpredictable. A surprise eruption in 1971 destroyed the **observatory** that was supposed to give warning of any surprise eruptions!

Rising up behind Florence are the Apennine Mountains, which run almost the whole length of the country. The Apennines are sometimes called the "spine of Italy."

Northern mountains

In the north are the Alps and Dolomites. These mountains are higher than the Apennines. In the north-west, Italy borders Mont Blanc, Europe's highest peak. The northern mountains are popular with climbers and walkers in summer, and skiers and snowboarders in winter.

The Tiber River flows past St Peter's **Basilica** (in the background) and under many ancient bridges in Rome.

Mount Etna is still dangerous. As recently as 1979, nine people died on the edge of the main **crater**.

WORD BANK   basilica building used as a law court or assembly hall in the Roman Empire
crater funnel-shaped hole inside the top of a volcano

Rivers

Waters from the Alps, Dolomites, and the northern edge of the Apennines all flow into Italy's greatest river, the Po. The Po River flows east to the Adriatic Sea. Its valley contains very good land for farming.

Near by your hotel flows another of Italy's rivers, the Arno. The Arno River can only be used by ships for the last 30 kilometres (18.6 miles) or so to the sea. The Arno Valley is famous for its vineyards and olive groves.

The Tiber River is one of the longest in Italy at 405 kilometres (252 miles). It flows through Rome to the sea, and has been made famous in many plays and stories about the city.

The dry weather in the south means the rivers are quite small. Some even dry up completely during the hottest weather.

Snowboard heaven!

Alberto Schiavon is one of Italy's top snowboarders. He lives in the Alto-Adige region, in the town of Madonna di Campiglio. "I have two lives", he says. "In one life I am doing **freeriding**. My second life is being part of the national team . . . it's the only way to reach the Olympics."

➤ Today, young Italians are just as likely to take up snowboarding as skiing.

freeriding snowboarding on whatever route you choose
observatory lookout or observation post

Weather in Italy

Open for business

Most shops and businesses in Italy open at 9 a.m., then close during the hottest part of the day from about 1 p.m. until 4 p.m. They reopen until about 7:30 p.m. in the evening. Almost everything closes on Sundays!

In June, when the *Gioco di Calcio Storico* kicks off, northern Italy is usually dry and hot. Watching the football match must have been a hot and sweaty experience, unless you found a bit of shade!

In the north, average temperatures reach over 20 °C (68 °F) in June. The region stays this warm until September. Winters can be miserably cold, with temperatures of 5–6 °C (41–42.8 °F). There are plenty of rainy days, and the **plains** sometimes suffer from freezing winds. In the northern mountains there is a lot of snow in winter. Further south, only the highest peaks ever see snow in winter.

Even during winter, the weather in Sicily is enjoyably warm. This is one of Italy's smartest resorts, Taormina in Sicily.

14   **WORD BANK**   plain high, flat area of land

Southern weather

In southern Italy, the summer weather is similar to that in the north. The temperature drops during winter, but nothing like as much as the north. If you travel to the south in the winter, a light jacket will usually be warm enough. In Palermo, for example, the average temperature rarely drops below 10 °C (50 °F). Even in winter, rain and cold weather are very unlikely.

Temperatures around Italy

This table shows the different temperatures across Italy.

City:	July temp.	January temp.
Bologna	26 °C / 79 °F	2.5 °C / 36.5 °F
Florence	25 °C / 77 °F	5.6 °C / 42.8 °F
Milan	24.8 °C / 76 °F	1.9 °C / 35.4 °F
Palermo	25.3 °C / 77.5 °F	10.3 °C / 50.5 °F
Rome	25.7 °C / 78.2 °F	7.4 °C / 45.3 °F

Wherever you are in the world, few people enjoy cold, rainy days like this one!

Food & culture

Food words

These are a few food words that a traveller in Italy might find handy:

bread *pane*

eggs *uova*

rice *riso*

fish *pesce*

soup *zuppa*

shellfish *crostacei*

meat *carne*

vegetables *contorni*

pasta *pasta*

All that watching football is hungry work. It's time to get something to eat! What might you find on the menu in Italy? The different regions are very proud of their own styles of cooking. But there are plenty of foods that are popular throughout the country, too.

Snacks

For a lunchtime snack, Italians often pick up *panini* (sandwiches) or slices of hot pizza. You decide to try a slice of pizza, to see if it is different here from the pizza at home. The man who sells it to you says that he is from Naples, in the south. This is where pizza comes from, too!

Pizza is enjoyed around the world and is still a favourite in Italy – where it comes from!
▶

16

Eating out

If you wanted a bigger meal, you would need to go to a *trattoria*. A *trattoria* usually opens for lunch and dinner. A *ristorante* will only open for dinner, except in larger towns where it will also open in the evening. In the countryside, eating in a *trattoria* can be quite an adventure. They often have no menu. The waiter just tells you what's being cooked today, and you pick what sounds best. Whatever you choose is almost always delicious!

Eating together

Italian families love eating together at home. They often spend hours preparing the food for family get-togethers. The meal can last a long time, with four or more courses.

"Fat Bologna"

Bologna is famous throughout Italy for its fine food. The city is even sometimes called *"Bologna la Grassa"* – Bologna the Fat! Bolognese sauce is now famous around the world, but you never see it on menus in the city. Instead, it is called *ragu*.

Italy's warm climate is perfect for eating outside.

Scooter crazy

Italy must be the scooter capital of the world! Scooters are a great way to get around the crowded, narrow streets of Italy's cities. Many people get one as soon as they are old enough.

Out and about

After all that wandering around in the heat, then your lunch, you must feel like a nap. Don't worry – almost everyone else will be taking one, too!

By the time you wake up, it is early evening. Florentines, like most other Italians, are starting to think about the *passeggiata*. This is a **ritual** all over Italy. People go out in the cool evening for a wander up and down the main street. They often stop to chat with their friends. People of all ages take part, from grandmothers to young children. Older children often go on their bikes and scooters.

Italy is the home of Vespa, the world's most famous maker of scooters.

WORD BANK   ritual regular event that people think is important

The *passeggiata* is a great way for people to see their friends. It is a chance to keep up with what is going on in your town or village. It is much more interesting than sitting in front of the television!

Clothes and fashion

People also like to use the *passeggiata* as a chance to show off their latest clothes. Many Italians take a lot of pride in the way they dress. Throughout Europe, they are known for being fashionably dressed. Have you packed anything trendy enough for the *passeggiata*?

Armani

Long before Giorgio Armani was a famous designer, he worked in a shop in Italy's fashion capital, Milan. Since then, Armani has made costumes for films such as *The Untouchables*, as well as clothes for film stars (and ordinary people, too)!

People of all ages meet up during the evening *passeggiata*.

The Siena Palio

Just a short drive from Florence is the town of Siena. Every year riders and horses from different districts of the city race around the central square. The races are called the *Palio*, and they attract huge crowds.

Festivals

Italy is a Roman Catholic country. The headquarters of the Roman Catholic religion is in Rome. Throughout the year there are many religious festivals, often in honour of **patron saints**. The *Gioco di Calcio Storico* football game you watched this morning is part of the Festival of St John, for example.

Usually festivals start with a **procession**, then there is a religious service. After this, there is some sort of celebration. There will be music, dancing, and plenty of food and drink!

The *Palio* goes around a very tight circuit, and is one of the world's most dangerous horse races.

WORD BANK   patron saint   saint linked with a particular place, job, or activity
procession   group of people marching in a ceremony

Pilgrimages

Pilgrimages are popular with many religious Italians. Often these involve a tough climb to visit a shrine on a hilltop. In the Aspromonte mountains of Calabria, for example, worshippers make the long climb to the shrine of the Madonna di Polsi.

Non-religious festivals

Not all Italy's festivals are religious. Some celebrate local history, and others are linked to music, painting, or film. Every year, filmmakers from around the world enter their films in the Venice film festival, for example. If you visit Venice in late August, you might even spot a film star or two!

Alternatively, you might be lucky enough to stumble on a local food festival. These usually celebrate a local **speciality**. In Alba, for example, there is a **truffle** festival every October.

Sagra di San Nicola

In the southern city of Bari, the procession for the *Sagra di San Nicola* festival is unusual. People in boats follow a boat carrying an image of the saint out to sea. Then they have a ceremony to honour a group of sailors who once saved the saint's bones from thieves.

Participants in Alba's truffle festival, held in October, wear **medieval** costumes and perform for the spectators.

truffle very tasty underground fungus, a bit like a mushroom

People in Italy

Holiday fact file

These are the days when almost everyone in Italy takes a day off:

1 JANUARY – New Year's Day

6 JANUARY – Epiphany, a Christian festival

EASTER MONDAY – a Christian festival

25 APRIL – Liberation Day, celebrating Italy's liberation (freedom) from German **occupation** during World War II

See p. 23 for more holidays...

There is one great Italian festival that starts in August and carries on every Sunday afternoon until May. Its name? The football season! It's not a real festival, of course, but football is very, very popular in Italy.

The big-city teams have passionate fans. Matches between two teams from the same area always generate lots of excitement. The matches between AC Milan and Inter Milan, or Roma and Lazio (both from Rome) are always important games. The crowds of fans are good-natured, even though the rivalry is fierce.

Sunday afternoon *Serie A* matches between Italy's top football teams are always colourful!

occupation when one country's army enters and takes control of another country

Road racing

During the summer, when the football season is finished, many Italians turn their attention to cycling. The *Giro d'Italia* is a race around Italy that draws thousands of cycling fans.

Motor racing is also a popular spectator sport. The fans are called *tifosi*. They follow Ferrari, as well as the brilliant motorcycle racers Valentino Rossi and Max Biaggi.

Theatre and cinema

Italians also love going to the theatre and cinema when they have free time. This is often a good excuse to eat out as well!

More holidays

1 MAY – Labour Day

15 AUGUST – Feast of the Assumption, another Christian festival

1 NOVEMBER – All Saints Day

8 DECEMBER – Feast of the Immaculate Conception, a Christian festival

25 AND 26 DECEMBER – Christmas Day and Boxing Day

One of the most successful Italian cyclists ever, Mario Cipollini (right), sprints towards the finish in the *Giro d'Italia*.

School

Of course, for all the time you are in Italy you do not have to go to school! What about your Italian friends? What is school like for them?

Italian children have to start school by six years old. Most start sooner – 96 percent of children go to school between the ages of three and five. They must stay at school until they are fifteen. The government plans to extend this to eighteen.

The school day

In the past, school stopped for 2 hours in the middle of the day. Children would go home and have lunch with their family. Now, many parents are working and it is difficult for everyone to get home. Today, children can stay at school for lunch.

Languages

School lessons are normally in Italian. But in some regions, Italian is not the main language. Schools in these areas can teach lessons in other languages:

- Trentino-Alto Adige: German
- Aosta Valley: French
- Trieste and Gorizia: Slovene

► Schoolchildren in Italy do not usually have to wear a uniform.

WORD BANK   mechanization use of machines instead of human workers

Work

Most Italians now live in cities. These people have jobs just like city-dwellers elsewhere. They work in offices, shops, or factories.

In the countryside, some people still work on farms. But **mechanization** has meant fewer jobs. Also, people are drawn to the cities and towns. They like the higher wages available in the city. They also enjoy the restaurants, theatres, cinemas, sports centres, and other attractions in cities.

The Fiat car factory in Turin. Fiat is one of Italy's biggest employers.

City-dwellers

Just over 67 percent of Italians lived in cities or towns in the year 2000. This is quite low compared to some other wealthy countries:

Australia
91 percent

France
75 percent

Germany
88 percent

South Korea
82 percent

United Kingdom
89 percent

United States
77 percent

Life in the cities

You are here! ● ROME

N
W — E
S

0 ————— 150 km
0 ————— 100 miles

The saying "All roads lead to Rome" comes from the days of the Roman **Empire**. The ancient Romans were famous for the long, straight roads they built. Because Rome was at the heart of the Empire, all roads seemed eventually to lead straight there.

It is time for you to follow the ancient Romans to Italy's capital city, Rome. But you are not exactly following in their footsteps – it's too far to walk! Instead, you decide to take the train.

Ancient Rome was laid out around seven famous hills. Today Rome is much bigger and there are about twenty hills within the city.

Rome fact file

FOUNDED:
753 BC

POPULATION:
4 million

SEVEN HILLS OF ANCIENT ROME:
Aventine, Caelian, Capitoline, Esquiline, Palatine, Quirinal, and Viminal.

WORD BANK amphitheatre circular building with seats surrounding a central arena, used as a place for public contests in ancient Rome

Arriving in Rome

You arrive at the *Stazione Termini*, where the train leaves you right in the heart of the city. Next, you climb the Esquiline Hill, one of the seven hills of ancient Rome. From up here, you will see the Tiber River winding through the city. Off to the north-west you can see the Vatican City in the distance.

Everywhere in Rome there are buildings that remind people of ancient times. Most impressive of all, at the foot of the Esquiline Hill, is the Colosseum. Here the rulers of Rome would put on contests to entertain people. Its **amphitheatre** was huge – up to 50,000 spectators would pack inside to watch the duelling **gladiators**.

Catacombs

Catacombs are underground burial tunnels. Early Christians built Rome's catacombs between AD 200 and 300. The catacombs spread over 240 hectares (600 acres). Under Roman law, places of burial were **sacred** and could not be attacked. So the Christians also used the catacombs to hide from their enemies.

The Colosseum is one of Rome's most famous sights. In ancient times, gladiators would fight to the death in front of huge crowds here.

gladiator   man who was forced to fight in public contests in ancient Rome
sacred   holy, religious

Italian cities

Rome today is a busy, crowded city. As you walk along its streets, traffic jams of cars crawl by. At the front of every queue is a swarm of scooters. When the traffic lights turn green, they're off, zipping in and out of the traffic. This is definitely the fastest way to get around the city!

The pavements are lined with shops and cafes. People enjoy a quick coffee or a pastry on their way to work. Many people work in government offices. About 600,000 of the city's 4 million people work in an office of some sort.

San Gennaro's miracle

Each year, Naples Cathedral hosts the miracle of San Gennaro. A **vial** of the saint's blood is taken out of storage. At the start of the ceremony, the blood is solid. By the end, it has miraculously turned to liquid. Over the next week, worshippers queue to kiss the vial, before it is taken back to storage.

Milan is Italy's fashion capital. This is where many of the world's most famous designers are based. But the city suffers from summertime **pollution**. Many of its buildings are new and very plain.

Unlike Milan, the centre of Turin is full of beautiful old buildings. The Fiat car company built many of Turin's **suburbs** to house its workers.

Milan

Turin

Florence

Rome

Naples

N
W   E
S

0   150 km

0   100 miles

Palermo

Naples is a big city — noisy and full of traffic. The combined noise, crowds, buildings, and local people make it unlike anywhere else in Italy. The old centre of the city, the centro storico, is full of street sellers and food stalls.

pollution release of harmful chemicals into the air, ground, or water
suburb area of homes on the outskirts of a city

What are Italy's other big cities like, and why might you decide to visit them?

- Cagliari has a rich history, which tourists can enjoy against a backdrop of year-round blue skies.
- Palermo blends African and European styles.
- Rome is Italy's capital and the headquarters of the Roman Catholic religion.

The first capital

Turin was Italy's first-ever capital city. The country's first king, Victor Emmanuel II, was from Turin. He was declared king in 1860. Turin's rule lasted only 10 years, though. In 1871, Rome became the new capital.

South of Naples, the beautiful Amalfi Coast is popular with holidaymakers from all over Europe.

Ancient traffic jams

Rome's traffic problems are not a new thing. Even in ancient Rome, when there were no cars or scooters around, one writer complained that noise from traffic passing in the streets kept him awake all night!

Urban life

The first things you notice about Rome are the ancient buildings that seem to be everywhere. The next thing you notice is the traffic! The streets are completely clogged with queues of cars with honking horns.

Monuments under threat

Rome's traffic problems are now so bad that **pollution** is affecting the ancient monuments. It eats away at the stone they are built from, and is slowly destroying them.

▶ In Italy, everyone seems to have a car, which can lead to some very busy roads!

30

Tough times in the city

Other Italian cities have traffic problems, though few are as bad as Rome's. There is also a shortage of homes in many cities, so people sometimes have to live crowded together. Around the edges of the cities there are some poor areas where people struggle to earn enough money to live on.

Fun in the city

Italians love to spend time with their friends. In the city, they still meet up for the *passeggiata*, an evening stroll with their family and friends. But there are also plenty of restaurants, cinemas, theatres, art galleries, and sports clubs.

Cars per person

Italian cities have a large number of cars per person – except Venice, where boats are more useful!

Turin	65 cars per 100 people
Venice	42.8 cars per 100 people
Bologna	56.9 cars per 100 people
Florence	56.8 cars per 100 people
Rome	68.4 cars per 100 people
Naples	60.4 cars per 100 people

Some buildings in Venice are so close together, that washing can be hung between them to dry!

Trains, planes, and cars

Judging by how busy the traffic is, you would think everyone in Italy went everywhere by road. The main roads linking Italy's cities are often excellent, especially in the north. But when it is time to leave Rome, what other ways of travelling will you find?

Trains

Italy's intercity trains are usually very good. There are even high-speed trains to the rest of Europe. Most of the international trains pass through tunnels that run deep beneath the Alps. They can whiz you to Vienna (in Austria), Geneva (in Switzerland), or Paris (in France) in just a few hours. From Italy's bigger cities, the local rail networks can take you to smaller towns and villages.

Water-buses

In Venice, instead of catching an ordinary bus, people catch *vaporetti* (water-buses). These bus-boats stop at docks all over the city, and are the easiest way to get around (see below).

A high-speed train whizzes through the beautiful Tuscan countryside.

Planes

When you leave Italy, you will be able to take an international flight from one of the big cities such as Milan, Rome, or Pisa.

Many airports in Italy's smaller towns and cities are getting busier all the time. They are often used by low-cost airlines. These airlines are able to offer cheaper flights because they do not have to pay the costs of flying into a large, big-city airport. Since the 1990s, these low-cost flights have brought many tourists to Italy.

Amalfi Coast

The winding road along the Amalfi Coast is one of the most famous roads in Italy. Every weekend it is busy with people racing along in flashy cars or on fast motorbikes. Some car manufacturers even bring journalists here to test-drive their new vehicles.

SWITZERLAND
AUSTRIA
Geneva
N
W   E
S
0   150 km
0   100 miles
Milan
Verona
Venice
Trieste
CROATIA
Turin
FRANCE
Genoa
Bologna
BOSNIA-HERZEGOVINA
Pisa
Florence
Marseilles
Siena
ADRIATIC SEA
SERBIA
Pescara
Rome
Bari
Dibia
Brindisi
SARDINIA
Naples
Taranto
Cagliari
TYRRHENIAN SEA

KEY
— Railroad
— Road
✈ Airport

Palermo
Messina
Reggio
Agrigento
SICILY
Siracusa
Tunis
ALGERIA
TUNISIA
MEDITERRANEAN SEA

It is easy to travel around Italy, whether you decide to travel by road, rail or air!

Countryside & coast

Simple pasta recipe

This recipe is enough for two people. It takes about 10 minutes to cook.

Ingredients:

• a tablespoon of dried porcini mushrooms

• four medium-sized fresh mushrooms

• two cups of trofi pasta

• a sprinkling of parmesan cheese

• a splash of olive oil

• a pinch of salt and pepper

(See p. 35 for the cooking instructions).

Even big cities like Rome have outdoor markets. Wandering into one of these, you see that the stalls sell an amazing variety of products. Most stalls have a **speciality** – cheese, meat, fish, fruit and vegetables, sweets, cakes, or bread.

People take great care choosing what they buy. They wander from stall to stall looking closely at what is on offer and who has the best prices. Much of this food is brought to the city straight from the Italian countryside and is very fresh.

Farming in Italy

Many Italian farms are smaller than elsewhere in Europe. Groups of farmers join together in a **cooperative**. This means that they can share the cost of preparing their crops for sale and transporting them to market. The largest farms are on the flat **plains** of Italy's river valleys, especially the Po valley in the north.

Hilly areas like Tuscany and Umbria are full of small, picturesque farms.

Italian food is popular all over the world. Italy **exports** olive oil, balsamic vinegar, sun-dried tomatoes, and dried porcini mushrooms, for example, to many other countries. Of course, one of the world's favourite Italian foods is pasta. Not all pasta is made in Italy, but plenty of it is still exported.

Get cooking!

1) Soak the porcini in water for 30 minutes

2) Put the pasta, a little olive oil, and salt into a pan of boiling water

3) Chop the fresh mushrooms into very small pieces, and the porcini into large ones

4) Fry the mushrooms and porcini in a splash of olive oil

5) Drain the pasta. Add butter, salt, and pepper to the pan. Then return the pasta to the pan.

6) Stir in the mushrooms and the porcini, sprinkle on the grated parmesan, stir again, and serve.

Italian pasta comes in many different shapes, sizes, and colours!

export when a country's produce is sold abroad

Mafia

By the mid-20th century the mafia had grown into an international crime organization. However, this was a long way from the humble beginnings of the group in rural Sicily. Local chiefs insisted that people had to pay to use the water wells they controlled. Those who did not pay could expect harsh punishments.

The south

In the south, life has not always been easy for small farmers. In the past, a farmer's land might be a long walk from his home in the village, and a long way from any water source. This made working on the land hard. The thin, dry soil in parts of the south was not as able to produce good crops as the north's river valleys.

Even today, many southern farmers have only very small plots of land and find it hard to make a good living from them. Many young people from the country move to the cities in search of a better lifestyle.

Calabria in the south is one of Italy's poorest regions. People still use donkeys and carts to get around.

WORD BANK   economy to do with money
rural to do with the countryside

New arrivals

Today, increasing numbers of people from elsewhere in Europe are buying **second homes** in the northern Italian countryside. Some foreigners are even moving there permanently. These newcomers bring money to the **rural economy**. The south's warm weather may also start to attract buyers from abroad in the future.

Price rises

The wealthy foreign buyers have caused house prices to rise. This sometimes means that young local people cannot afford to buy homes in the area where they have always lived. Instead, they move to the cities.

Festival of Forgotten Fruit

One of Italy's strangest rural food festivals is at Casola Valsenio in Ravenna. At the Festival of Forgotten Fruit you can try fruits that are no longer popular or sold in shops. Some of them are so unusual they have no name in English!

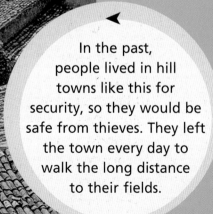

In the past, people lived in hill towns like this for security, so they would be safe from thieves. They left the town every day to walk the long distance to their fields.

second home house that people do not use as their main home

Fishing

One of the things you notice as you wander around the market in Rome is the huge variety of fish for sale. Among the unusual sights are slippery eels, garfish with pointy noses, squid, and octopus.

Italians love fish, and every year they eat more of it. In 1994, 50 Italians in every 100 ate fish at least once a day. By 2000, the figure had risen to 55 in every 100. Italy has a long coastline with plenty of fishing ports. Even so, there is so much demand for fish that Italy has to **import** it from elsewhere.

Cod-jackers!

The traditional Naples Christmas Eve meal of dried cod is under threat. Thieves keep stopping the lorries, which bring the cod from Norway, to steal their loads. Some Norwegian companies are now refusing to **export** their fish to Italy.

▶ Specialist fish markets, such as this one in Rome, sell huge varieties of fish and seafood.

Shellfish are especially popular – the menus in most restaurants include shellfish such as mussels, shrimps, or prawns. Italian fishermen also regularly bring tuna, sardines, and tiny, salty anchovies to market. Some of the fish for sale at the market are **freshwater** fish such as trout. Most fish, though, will come from the sea.

Liguria, in the north, and Puglia and Sicily, in the south, are the two areas of Italy most famous for seafood cooking, even though they are at opposite ends of the country.

Fishing for tuna

The *mattanza* is the way the fishermen of Favignana catch tuna. The tuna are trapped in a giant circular net. The fishermen then lean over to spear the fish on hooks attached to long wooden poles. The huge fish are then hauled into the boats.

Many animal-rights campaigners say the *mattanza* is cruel. Others claim that it is probably less cruel than using a hook and line or nets.

Tourism and travel

On your last day in Rome, you find a map someone has left behind on the seat of a bus. He or she must have been a traveller too, because they have made notes about the different places in Italy they have visited.

La Befana

The old woman *La Befana* was a good witch from long ago who loved children. Today, she is said to wander Italy on 5 January, leaving presents for youngsters. In Rome on 6 January, there is a toy fair in her honour.

Siena is said to be one of the most beautiful towns in Italy. The **medieval** centre is home to the *Palio* horse race, one of the country's most spectacular festivals.

The Leaning Tower of Pisa is one of Italy's most famous sights. It was built on sandy soil, which has caused it to lean over slowly through the years. Now the tilt is clearly visible! The tower stands in the *Campo dei Miracoli* – the Field of Miracles.

Pompeii and Herculaneum:
The volcano Mount Vesuvius, near Naples, destroyed these two ancient Roman towns in AD 79. Today, visitors come to see the remains of the towns, which were buried under ash and earth for hundreds of years before being uncovered.

There are more canals and boats in Venice than roads and cars. The city is very beautiful, but try to pick a quiet time to visit — up to 15 million tourists go there every year, and it can get very crowded!

Before the Roman Empire, the Greeks ruled parts of Sicily and southern Italy. The Greek temples at Agrigento were built in the 5th century BC, and there are no others like them except in Greece itself.

Stay, or go home?

So, you've seen a bit of Italy: the sights of Rome and Florence, and the Tuscan countryside in between. But perhaps the map you found has made you want to see more? Here are some suggestions for daredevil activities you might want to try before you head for home.

Via ferrata

Clamber along a *via ferrata* route in the Dolomite mountains. These combine walking and climbing, sometimes up iron ladders bolted to the rockface. Don't try this in a thunderstorm – the ladders become giant lightning conductors!

Via ferrata means iron road in Italian. Adventurers come from all over to climb these steep iron ladders.

WORD BANK   peninsula long, thin strip of land sticking out to sea

Snowboard Sestriére

What about trying your hand at snowboarding in Sestriére, one of Italy's top ski resorts? Or maybe you could watch the World Cup skiers race down the mountain?

Climb Mount Etna

How about a trip to Mount Etna in Sicily, one of the world's largest volcanoes at 3,325 metres (10,952 feet)? You can even walk up to the main **crater** (see right), where you will be surprised to find a cafe!

Surf Sardinia

The west coast of Sardinia is one of the best places in the Mediterranean for surfing. Head for the **peninsula** of Putzu Idu if you want to catch some Italian waves.

Windsurf on Lake Como

Even though it is a long way from the sea, Lake Como in the north of Italy is a favourite destination for windsurfers. They are drawn here by the winds that pick up along the lake as they whistle through the mountains.

So, what are you planning to do? Get on a plane and head for home, or stay and sample a bit more of Italy?

> Italy's northern lakes are home to some of Europe's best inland windsurfing.

Find out more

Destination Detectives can find out more about Italy by using the books, websites, and addresses listed below:

World Wide Web

If you want to find out more about Italy, you can search the Internet using keywords such as these:

- Italy
- River Po
- The European Union

You can also find your own keywords by using headings or words from this book. Try using a search directory such as **yahooligans.com**.

Movies

Roman Holiday (1953) One of the most famous films ever set in Rome. Audrey Hepburn and Gregory Peck have a great time whizzing around the city on a scooter.

The Italian Job (1969) Michael Caine leads a daring gang of robbers trying to steal a load of gold from the heart of Turin. This movie helped make Mini Cooper cars cool in the United Kingdom.

The Italian Embassy

The Italian Embassy in your country will be able to give you lots of information about Italy. Often the embassy will have information packs that they can send out about the best times to visit, special events, and Italian culture. The UK embassy address is:

Italian Embassy in London
14, Three Kings Yard
Davies Street
London W1K 2EH.

The embassy also has a useful website:

www.embitaly.org.uk

Further reading

The following books are packed with useful information about Italy:

Countries of the World: Italy, Sally Garrington (Facts on File, 2004)

Lonely Planet Phrasebook: Italian (Lonely Planet, 2001)

Take Your Camera: Italy, Ted Park (Raintree, 2004)

The Rough Guide To Italy , Martin Dunford (Rough Guides, 2005)

Timeline

753 BC
According to legend, Romulus and Remus found the city of Rome.

509 BC
Rome becomes a republic.

264–146 BC
Rome expands overseas during the Punic Wars.

27 BC
Augustus becomes the first Roman emperor.

96–180 AD
The Roman **Empire** reaches the height of its power.

395 AD
The Roman Empire splits into two parts, the West and East Roman Empire.

476 AD
The last emperor of the West Roman Empire, Romulus Augustulus, is overthrown by a tribe.

962
Otto the Great is crowned emperor, marking the start of what was later called the Holy Roman Empire.

1000
Italian city-states begin to get richer and more important.

around 1300
The Renaissance begins in Italy.

1519
King Charles I of Spain becomes emperor of the Holy Roman Empire.

1521–1559
The forces of Spain and the Holy Roman Empire defeat France in a series of wars to control Italy.

1796
Napoleon Bonaparte seizes Italy for France.

1814–1815
Italy is returned to its former rulers after Napoleon is defeated.

1861
The Kingdom of Italy is formed.

1866
Venetia becomes part of Italy.

1870
Rome becomes part of Italy.

1871
Rome becomes the capital of Italy.

1915–1918
Italy fights on the side of the **Allies** in World War I.

1922
Benito Mussolini becomes prime minister.

1936
Italy conquers Ethiopia.

1940
Italy enters World War II on Germany's side.

1943
Italy surrenders to the Allies.

1946
The Republic of Italy is established.

1980
An earthquake strikes southern Campania and Basilicata, killing over 4,500 people.

Italy – facts & figures

Italy's flag was first used in 1796 when Italy was still part of the French Empire. Napoleon Bonaparte was once general of the French Revolution and later the leader of both France and Italy. He designed the Italian flag to look like the French Flag, but apparently changed the French blue to his favourite colour, green!

People and places

- Population: 57.4 million.
- Italians were known for having large families. However, Italy is now known for having Europe's lowest birth rate.
- Average life expectancy: 78.2 years

What's in a name?

- Italy's name comes from the ancient Roman word *Italia*, meaning land of oxen or grazing land. Italy's official name is *Reppulica Italiana*.

Money matters

- Before adopting the euro, Italy's currency was the *lira*.
- Italy is the world's fifth largest industrial economy.
- Average earnings:
Men – £18,230 (US$33,084)
Women – £8,142 (US$14,719)

Food facts

- The average Italian consumes 227 grams (about half a pound) of bread a day!
- The ice-cream cone is an Italian invention.
- The national dish is pasta, and the average Italian is said to eat a whopping 25 kilograms (55 pounds) of pasta a year.

Glossary

Allies France, Russia, the British Empire, United States, and Italy who fought together in World War I

amphitheatre circular building with seats surrounding a central arena, used as a place for public contests in ancient Rome

architect person whose job it is to design buildings

assassinate to kill or murder someone

basilica building used as a law court or assembly hall in the Roman Empire

cooperative organization that is owned by everyone who works within it

crater funnel-shaped hole inside the top of a volcano

democracy where the people of a country elect their government

dictator ruler who has complete power over everyone and everything

economy to do with money

empire group of countries controlled by another country

execution killing of someone on the orders of the government or a ruler

export when a country's produce is sold abroad

freeriding snowboarding on whatever route you choose

gladiator man who was forced to fight in public contests in ancient Rome

import buy from another country

mechanization use of machines instead of human workers

medieval period from between about AD 500 and 1500

monk man who lives in a religious community, devoting his life to religion

nationalist someone who wants his or her country to have its own government

observatory lookout or observation post

occupation when one country's army enters and takes control of another country

patron saint saint linked with a particular place, job, or activity

peninsula long, thin strip of land sticking out into the sea

pilgrimage journey that a person makes to a holy place

plague disease that spreads quickly and affects a lot of people

plain high, flat area of land

pollution release of harmful chemicals into the air, ground, or water

procession group of people marching in a ceremony

ritual regular event that people think is important

rural to do with the countryside

sacred holy, religious

saliva watery liquid produced in your mouth

second home house that someone does not use as their main home

speciality food from a particular place

suburb area of homes on the outskirts of a city

truffle very tasty underground fungus, a bit like a mushroom

vial glass container for liquids

Index